Contents

Contents

Introduction: What is the Moon?

Look up into the sky on any cloudless night, and chances are you'll see the Moon. Our glowing neighbor in space is as familiar to us as the Sun and the stars. You may even have imagined walking on its surface. But how much do you really know about the Moon? You may already know that the Moon is our planet's only natural satellite, that it circles the Earth, and that we can watch it go through phases from round and full to thin like a sickle. But do you know how high you could jump on the Moon? Or what the Moon's seas are made of? Or what would happen if we didn't have the Moon? (Hint: Our days would be a lot shorter.) Or how about whether people will ever visit the Moon again? Read on to find the answers to these fascinating questions and much more!

The man in the moon came down too soon and asked his way to Norwich. He went by the south and burned his mouth while supping cold pease porridge. — Traditional

Why is the Moon called the Moon?

The word *moon* comes from the old English word mōna, which comes from an ancient root word meaning "to measure." The word *month* comes from this same root.

In the legends of Native Americans, the Sun and the Moon are husband and wife. The Sun is fierce and, as he is always hungry, he wants to eat their children, the stars. Little stars stay with their caring mother, the Moon, at night and when their father, the Sun, wakes up, they run away. So the Moon can only come out and play with her little children at night.

People sometimes use the Latin name Luna for our moon. Luna was the Roman goddess of the Moon. This is where the word *lunar* comes from. We use this word to describe things related to the Moon—like lunar rocks, lunar craters, and the lunar calendar.

This is fitting, as humans throughout history have used the Moon's cycles to help them measure and keep track of time. Other languages have their own names for the Moon. In French, the Moon is called Lune. In Hindi, it's Chaand. And in Japanese, it's Tsuki.

The Moon is Earth's natural satellite. What is a satellite?

Answer:

A satellite is an object that orbits, or circles around, a celestial body like a planet or a star. Satellites are held in their orbits by the force of gravity. Some satellites travel in circular paths, while others have long orbits in the shape of an egg or a stretched-out rubber band. Did you know that you're on a satellite now? Earth and the other planets in our Solar System are satellites of the Sun, just like the Moon is a satellite of Earth.

Why is the Moon called a natural satellite? Does Earth have any unnatural satellites?

The Moon is called Earth's natural satellite because it was formed through natural processes and was not made by humans. There are also many human-made, or artificial, satellites, in orbit around Earth. Artificial satellites are machines that scientists build and launch into space. They have a variety of functions, including helping our phones, TV, and internet work over long distances, helping scientists track storms and study our atmosphere and oceans, and helping astronomers learn more about the universe. An example of this last kind of satellite is the Hubble Space Telescope. The International Space Station, an orbiting laboratory where scientists from many countries live and conduct experiments, is also an artificial satellite.

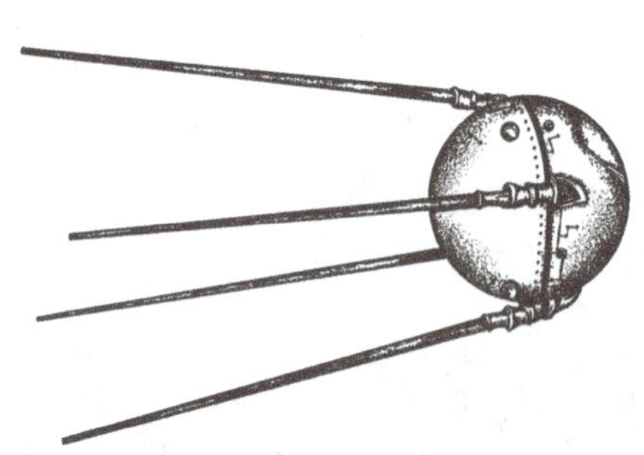

The first artificial satellite was a little ball of metal called Sputnik. Scientists in the Soviet Union built and launched it in 1957. Since then more than 8,000 satellites have been launched by dozens of countries across the world. More than half of these satellites are still in orbit around Earth. You've probably seen some of them in the night sky. They look like stars, but if you watch them closely, you'll notice that they are moving slowly.

Can you believe that the Earth has one more moon? The Moon was discovered in 1999. It is just three miles across. It is called Cruithne, and only a small number of people know about it.

What other planets have satellites?

Earth is not the only planet with natural satellites. In fact, except for Mercury and Venus, all the other planets in our Solar System have moons of their own. Some of them have dozens of moons, and scientists are constantly discovering more.

Mars, the fourth planet from the Sun, has two natural satellites called Phobos and Deimos. Both are lumpy, rocky, potato-shaped moons that are much smaller than Earth's moon—Deimos is only about 9 miles (15 km) across. Some scientists think they may have been asteroids that were captured by Mars's gravity.

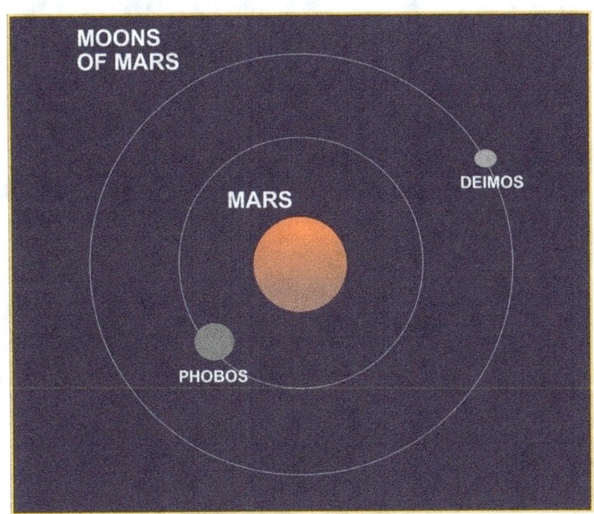

Jupiter is the largest planet in the Solar System, and it also has the most moons: so far, scientists have discovered 79! Can you imagine what our night sky would look like with that many moons? The largest four moons of Jupiter are named Europa, Callisto, Ganymede, and Io. These fascinating satellites are very different from Earth's moon. Europa and Callisto have icy surfaces, and scientists think there may be oceans of water beneath their surfaces. It's even possible that extraterrestrial life might exist there! Ganymede is the biggest moon in the Solar System. With a diameter of about 3,270 miles (5,260 km), it's even bigger than the planet Mercury. And Io is covered in active volcanoes that spew sulfur, making it look a little like a cheese pizza. ▶

Saturn is another planet with a lot of satellites: 62 in all. One of its most unique moons is named Titan. In some ways, Titan is a little bit like Earth. If you were standing on its surface, you'd see clouds in the sky and rivers and lakes all around you. You might be tempted to take a swim—but think again! Titan's rivers and lakes are made of freezing, cold, liquid methane.

Uranus has 27 moons, mostly named after characters from William Shakespeare's plays. Its largest moons are Titania, Oberon, Umbriel, Ariel, and Miranda. These are rocky, icy satellites covered in craters. Neptune, the far-

thest planet from the Sun, has 13 known satellites. Its largest moon, Triton, has icy volcanoes that spew out nitrogen gas instead of lava.

Finally, the dwarf planet Pluto has five moons. The largest of them, Charon, was named after the boatman who ferried souls across the river of the dead in Greek mythology. It's a fitting name for this cold, distant, and mysterious moon.

Of all the moons in the Solar System our moon is the fifth largest of all.

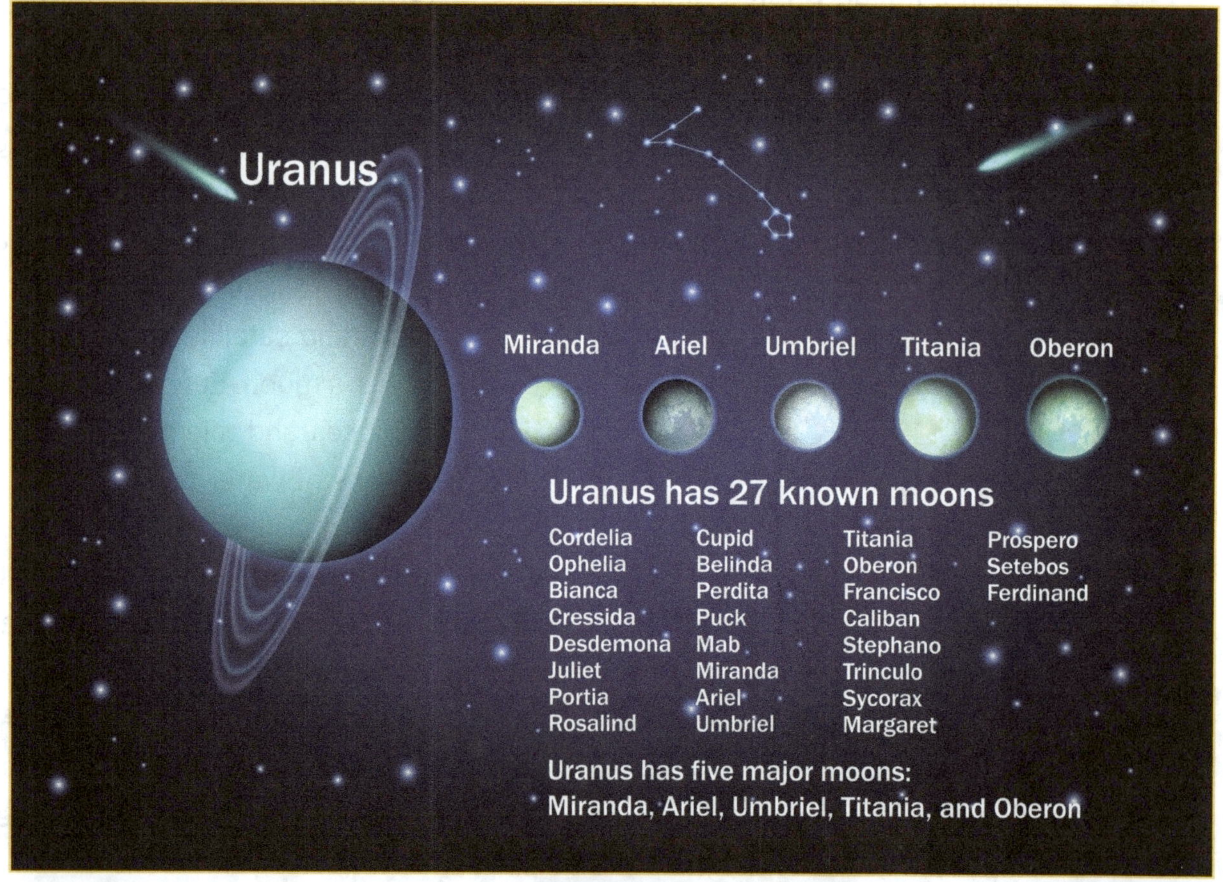

Does Earth have any other natural satellites besides the Moon?

Not really. The Moon is our only true natural satellite. However, you might be surprised to learn that small asteroids sometimes circle Earth temporarily. These asteroids actually orbit the Sun, not Earth, but their long, elliptical paths bring them close to Earth. When this happens, Earth's gravity can capture them for a short time before they break free and continue on their way. For example, in 2006, scientists discovered a tiny asteroid they named 2006 RH120. This asteroid, which was only a few feet across, circled Earth for almost a year and then wandered away. Think of asteroids like these as guests who visit for a short time before heading off again. Our Moon, though, is here to stay.

Can we call the Moon a planet?

No. Even though it's massive and round, the Moon doesn't fit the definition of a planet. The International Astronomical Union (IAU) is a group of scientists who make decisions about the terms we use to describe planets, moons and other objects in our universe. The IAU lists several conditions that must be met in order for a celestial body to be called a planet. One of these rules is that the body must orbit around the Sun. The Moon orbits Earth, not the Sun, so it cannot be a planet. The Moon could only become a planet if it somehow broke free of Earth's gravity and entered into its own orbit around the Sun, but we definitely wouldn't want that!

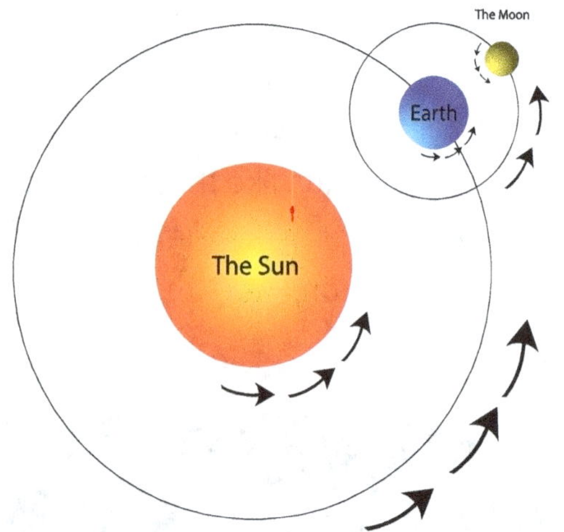

The Moon makes a circle around Earth within 27 days, 7 hours, 43 minutes and 11.6 seconds.

Why doesn't the Moon fall to the Earth or fly into open space?

The Moon stays in its orbit because of two important things—Earth's gravity and the Moon's speed. Gravity is a force that makes massive objects in space, like the Moon and Earth, pull on each other. It's because of Earth's strong gravity that the Moon doesn't fly away into space. If the Moon weren't moving, gravity would pull it into Earth, causing a gigantic crash (and a huge mess). However, because the Moon is traveling very fast, it stays in its orbit and circles around Earth. ▶

I magine that you are holding a ball on a string and spinning it around you while you stand still. You're like Earth, and the ball is like the Moon. The string is like gravity, keeping the ball from flying away from you, and because the ball is traveling sideways very fast, it stays in the air instead of falling down.

Question:

Why doesn't the Moon have satellites?

Answer:

T he Moon has no smaller moons circling it. This is because Earth's gravity is so strong that it would pull any natural satellite out of the Moon's orbit or cause it to crash into the Moon. The Moon would have to be a lot farther away from Earth to keep its own moon in orbit around it. The Moon does, however, have several artificial satellites circling it. One of them, called the Lunar Reconnaissance ▶

Orbiter, was launched by the National Aeronautics and Space Administration (NASA), the United States' space agency, in 2009. It takes photographs to help scientists learn more about the Moon's surface.

None of the other moons in our Solar System have natural satellites either, as far as we know. But that doesn't mean it's impossible. Somewhere in the universe, there might be a planet with a moon that has its own moon. That would certainly look interesting in the sky. What would you call the moon of a moon?

How did the Moon appear in the sky?

Answer:

For as long as humans have been gazing up at the night sky, the Moon has been shining down. It's so familiar that we often don't think about it. But where did the Moon come from? We don't know for sure, but scientists have several hypotheses, or best guesses.

One thing we know for certain is that the Moon is very, very old. Astronauts who walked on the Moon brought rocks and soil from the surface back to Earth. By studying the chemicals in these rock samples, scientists have calculated that the Moon is about 4.5 billion years old. That's almost as old as Earth, so the Moon must have formed around the

same time as our planet and the rest of the Solar System. ▶

The early Solar System was a busier, messier place that it is today. There were lots of planets, asteroids and other objects crossing paths as they orbited the Sun. Most scientists think that the Moon formed when a small planet called Theia crashed into the Earth, causing a huge explosion. Broken fragments of Earth and Theia clumped together and formed the Moon. This is called the giant-impact hypothesis. It must have been a violent and dramatic time. Luckily for us humans, this happened billions of years before we came around.

Another possibility is that the Moon formed at the same time as Earth, out of the same cloud of dust and gas. Or, the Moon might have formed somewhere else in the Solar System before it was captured by Earth's gravity, but neither of these theories explains what scientists know about the rocks of the Moon as well as the giant-impact hypothesis.

What does the Moon look like? What is its size and weight?

You've seen the Moon plenty of times when you've looked up at the night sky—it looks like a pale circle (or sometimes a half-circle or crescent) dappled with dark splotches, about the size of the end of your thumb. But how big is the Moon really?

The Moon is actually a rocky, cratered sphere about 2,160 miles (3,475 km) in diameter. The Moon's circumference--the distance you would travel if you started at one point on the Moon's surface and walked all the way around it until you reached your starting point again--is about 6,780 miles (10,915 km). That's about the distance from New York City to Tokyo, and it's a little over one-fourth ▶

the size of Earth. If Earth were the size of a basketball, the Moon would be a bit smaller than a baseball. Technically, the Moon doesn't weigh anything at all, because it's in space! However, we can talk about the Moon's mass, which is a measure of the amount of rock and other material inside it. Compared to Earth, the Moon is not very massive. If you had a gigantic scale (use your imagination here) and put Earth on one side of it, it would take more than 80 Moons to balance it out.

What is on the Moon? Are there lunar cities and countries?

While it's fun to think about cities and countries on the Moon, there aren't any. As far as we know, nothing lives on the Moon. It's a dry, barren, lifeless place. But that doesn't mean it isn't remarkable in its own way.

If you were standing on the Moon, you'd see craters, plains, and mountains. Craters are deep circular pits left when meteors or asteroids strike the surface of the Moon. The Moon is covered in craters because, unlike Earth, it doesn't have an atmosphere to burn up smaller meteors and keep them from hitting its surface. It also doesn't have water, wind, or any of the other natural processes that cover Earth's craters over time. Once a crater is made on the Moon, it's there to stay. The largest and oldest lunar crater, called the Aitken Basin, is on the far side of the Moon (the side that always faces away from Earth), near the Moon's south pole. This gigantic crater is about 1,550 miles (2,500 km) across. That's about half the distance across the United States. Scientists think it was created when a very big rock slammed into the Moon almost 4 billion years ago. In 2019, Chinese scientists sent a spacecraft named Chang'e-4 to the Aitken Basin, where it became the first spacecraft ever to land on the far side of the Moon. ▶

Another well-known lunar crater is called Tycho. This crater is only about 108 million years old—very young compared to everything else on the Moon. Tycho is near the south pole of the Moon on the side facing Earth. You can see it yourself with your naked eye or using a pair of binoculars. It looks like a small circle with bright streaks of dust spidering out from it.

mountain, but if you measure the distance from this point to the average elevation of the lunar surface, the Selenean Summit is higher than Mount Everest!

There are also lunar lowlands—vast, smooth plains made of darker rock than the highlands and mountains. Astronomers call the plains on the Moon "seas." Read on to find out why.

The Moon also has highlands, mountains, and mountain ranges. The tallest mountain on the Moon is called Mons Huygens. It measures about 18,000 feet (5.5 km) from base to peak, which is almost as tall as Mount Denali, one of the highest peaks on Earth. There is an even higher point on the Moon called the Selenean Summit. It's a plateau, not a

The highest mountain on the Moon is Mons Huygens. It is 15 420 feet tall which is half of the height of Mt. Everest. Because the gravitational pull is nearly 83% less than on Earth, you can easily float to the top of Mons Huygens Mountain!

What are the Moon's seas? Can we swim in them?

You can't swim in the seas on the Moon—not even if you had a space-suit to protect you. That's because these "seas" are made of rock, not water. Early astronomers noticed that certain areas on its surface were a darker gray color than the surrounding regions. They called these dark splotches *maria*, which is Latin for "seas," because they believed at the time there might be oceans on the Moon. Actually, the dark areas are smooth, low plains made of basalt, a kind of rock. The lunar seas formed between 3 and 4 billion years ago, when the Moon was still young. Volcanic eruptions or impacts from meteors caused lava to flow over the Moon's surface and cool and harden into basalt. You can see the Moon's seas without a telescope—just look for the darker spots on its surface. Many people think the pattern made by the seas looks like a face, the "Man in the Moon." Others think it looks like a rabbit. What does it look like to you?

How many seas are there on the Moon?

Answer:

There are 23 *maria*, or seas, on the Moon. Almost all of them are on the near side of the Moon. Together, the seas cover about 16 percent of the Moon's total surface. The largest of the seas is called *Oceanus Procellarum*, or the Ocean of Storms. Despite its name, this isn't an ocean you can swim or sail in, and there aren't any storms there. Like the other lunar seas, it's a vast plain of smooth basalt. The Ocean of Storms is about 1,800 miles (2,900 km) across and can be seen along the western side of the Moon as viewed from Earth. Some of the other large *maria* are *Mare Frigoris* (Sea of Cold), *Mare Imbrium* (Sea of Shadows), *Mare Fecunditatis* (Sea of Fertility), and *Mare Tranquillitatis* (Sea of Tranquility). The last of these is famous for being the landing site of the Apollo 11 mission in 1969; it's where Neil Armstrong and Buzz Aldrin took their first steps on the Moon.

What is the far side of the Moon? Why do we never see it? What if that's where all the fun is?

The far side of the Moon (sometimes called the "dark side") is the side that always faces away from us when we view the Moon from Earth. Why doesn't the Moon ever turn around to show us its other side? The Moon is what scientists call tidally locked with Earth. That means that the Moon rotates at the very same rate that it orbits Earth. In other words, it completes one rotation on its own axis in the same time that it completes one full circle around our planet. The result is that the same side of the Moon always faces us.

Imagine that you're holding hands with your best friend and spinning them around in circles. As you spin, you'll always see your friend's face, never the back of their head. While this isn't a perfect analogy, it may help you to picture how the Moon looks from Earth.

The far side of the Moon used to be mysterious. Today, though, we know what the far side looks like because humans have sent satellites there to take photographs. It turns out that the far side is a lot like the near side, except that it has more craters and fewer seas. The largest crater on the Moon, the Aitken Basin, is on the far side.

What is the surface of the Moon like? Is it dusty?

Yes, very. The surface of the Moon is covered in a layer of dust, pebbles and broken rocks. This layer of debris is called lunar regolith. If you were to walk on the Moon, you would leave footprints, and the dust would cling to your boots and spacesuit. Regolith was formed as meteorites, and charged particles from the Sun broke down the rocks on the Moon's surface over billions of years. Unlike soil on Earth, which contains moisture and organic material (from decomposed plants and animals), the Moon's soil is dry and contains only rock and minerals.

Craters appeared on the Moon over 4 billion years ago. They were formed by asteroids, which fell on the Moon, and since then the craters have been unchanged because there is no geological activity and weather on the Moon.

What would happen if plant seeds were brought to the Moon? Would they grow into moon trees?

You could bring seeds from Earth to the Moon and plant them, but nothing would grow. This is because plants (at least the kind we have on our planet) need several things in order to grow and live: sunlight, carbon dioxide from the air, nutrients from the soil, water, and a temperature that isn't too hot or too cold. There is sunlight on the Moon—but as for the rest of the list, a plant on the Moon would be out of luck! There is no air on the Moon and very, very little water, and the lunar regolith doesn't have organic matter to provide nutrients. The temperatures on the Moon also vary widely. During the day, it gets too hot for plants to survive, and during the lunar night, they would freeze.

It might be possible to grow plants in lunar soil under certain conditions, however. Scientists in 2014 tried to do that in an experiment.[1] They took a lunar regolith simulant--a soil made from volcanic rock that looks and acts like soil on the Moon--and planted seeds in it. They exposed the seeds to air, gave them water, and controlled the temperature. The seeds did sprout and grow, showing that ▸

[1] Weiger Wamelink, G. W., J. Y. Frissel, W. H. J. Krijnen, M. R. Verwoert, and P. W. Goedhart. "Can Plants Grow on Mars and the Moon: A Growth Experiment on Mars and Moon Soil Simulants." PLOS One, 27 August 2014.

it might be possible for future astronauts to grow plants on the Moon in artificial, Earth-like conditions, such as under a protected dome.

Does the Moon have an atmosphere?

The answer is "sort of." The Moon's atmosphere is very, very thin. Scientists call it an exosphere, not a true atmosphere. The Moon does not have enough gravity to hold in gases and create a dense atmosphere. In fact, the Moon's exosphere is so thin it's not much different from the vacuum of empty space. Because of this, the sky on the Moon is always black, even in the daytime, not blue like it is on Earth. Gases in the Moon's faint "air" include argon, helium, neon, hydrogen, sodium, potassium, and other elements. These are gases that escaped from ▶

the Moon's interior or were released when solar wind or meteorites struck the moon's surface. Scientists believe that the Moon may have had a thicker atmosphere 3 or 4 billion years ago, when the Moon was young and volcanically active, but this atmosphere escaped into space. Needless to say, you can't breathe on the Moon. Astronauts visiting the Moon wore pressurized spacesuits and carried oxygen tanks.

Question:

Does it rain on the Moon?

Answer:

It never rains on the Moon, because the Moon doesn't have moisture or clouds in its extremely thin exosphere. That means you don't have to bring your umbrella if you're planning a trip there, but it also means that nothing can live or grow on the Moon. However, you might be surprised to learn that scientists *have* found evidence of water on the Moon! At least, a tiny bit of water. ▶

Scientists have detected water molecules here and there within the lunar soil. They've also found small amounts of ice in craters near the Moon's north and south poles. This isn't very much water – the Moon is still very, very dry – but it's exciting to think that future explorers on the Moon might be able to collect and make use of this water.

Do shadows on the Moon look scary?

If you were standing on the Moon during the daytime, you'd notice that your shadow looked sharper and darker than your shadow looks on Earth. The astronauts who visited the Moon struggled with shadows, because shadows sometimes made it hard for them to see their equipment. On Earth, the air scatters light, which usually makes shadows appear soft and translucent. The Moon, as you've learned, has no real atmosphere, so shadows look stark and black. That might be a little scary, but at least you could be confident there's nothing waiting in the shadows to jump out at you—except maybe one of your fellow astronauts playing a trick!

What are day and night like on the Moon? Are there sunrises and sunsets?

Like Earth, the Moon has days and nights. However, if you were living on the Moon, you'd find days and nights to be very different from what you're used to on our planet. For one thing, they're much longer. A full day on Earth, meaning the time it takes for Earth to spin around once on its axis, lasts about 24 hours. De-

pending on the season and where you live, that means roughly 12 hours of daylight and 12 hours of darkness. The Moon spins much more slowly. A full day on the Moon lasts about 29.5 Earth days! That means if you watched the sunrise on the Moon, it would take about two weeks for the Sun to set, and another two weeks for it to rise again. There are sunrises and sunsets on the Moon, but because the Moon has so little atmosphere, they aren't as pretty as they are on Earth—you wouldn't see pink and orange clouds or a colorful sky, and there's no twilight time just before sunrise or after sunset. Instead, the change from day to night (and vice versa) happens fairly quickly and completely.

Another difference you would notice (although hopefully you'd have a spacesuit to protect you) is that the temperature on the Moon changes drastically depending on whether it's day or night. During daylight hours, it gets very, very hot on the Moon—up to 260 degrees Fahrenheit (120 Celsius). That's hotter than the temperature at which water boils. At night, the temperature on the Moon falls to as low as -280 Fahrenheit (-170 Celsius). This is unimaginably cold—much colder than the lowest temperature ever recorded in Antarctica.

How long does a year on the Moon last?

The answer depends on what we mean by a year. If we define a year as the time it takes for the Moon to go around the Sun, then a year on the Moon lasts the same length as a year on Earth—about 365 Earth days. That's because Earth carries the Moon along with it in its orbit. If instead we define a year on the Moon as the time it takes the Moon to complete one full orbit around Earth, then a year on the Moon is about the same length as a day on the Moon—roughly two Earth weeks.

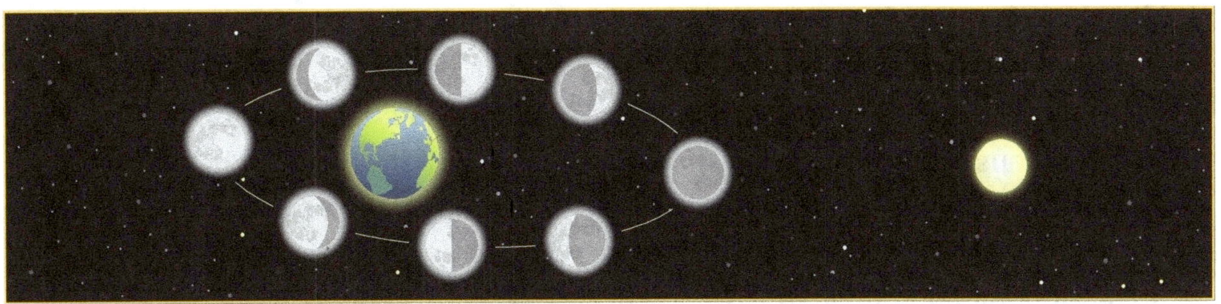

Do the seasons change on the Moon?

On Earth, we're used to having seasons—spring, summer, fall, and winter. Depending on where you live, there might be drastic differences between the temperature and weather outside as the seasons change. Seasons on Earth are caused by our planet's tilt on its axis, which is about 23.5 degrees. As Earth orbits the Sun, the hemisphere tilted toward the Sun receives more light and heat, causing it to be hotter there and cooler in the hemisphere tilted away. The Moon is also tilted on its axis, but its tilt is much less than Earth's. This means that you probably wouldn't notice seasons if you were living on the Moon. You *would* notice the dramatic change from hot daytime to cold nighttime, though.

There are earthquakes on Earth. Are there earthquakes on the Moon?

Answer:

Yes, and they happen a lot—but we call them moonquakes, naturally! Moonquakes have been measured by instruments that astronauts placed on the Moon's surface. Moonquakes are generally not as strong as quakes on Earth, but they can last much longer—up to several hours. This is because the Moon doesn't have water or other materials to absorb the energy from quakes once they've started. If a big quake happened while you were on the Moon, you might have to take shelter and wait a long time for the shaking to stop. On our planet, earthquakes are usually caused by tectonic plates—slabs of Earth's crust—shifting and scraping against each other. The Moon doesn't have tectonic plates. Its quakes are believed to be caused by the tidal pull from Earth's gravity, from the impact of meteorites, or from the Moon's crust expanding during the change from frigid nighttime to hot daytime.

Does the Moon have a magnetic field?

You may have heard of Earth's magnetic field, or magnetosphere—it's an invisible, magnetically-charged shield that surrounds Earth like a giant bubble and protects us from harmful solar wind, stellar flares and cosmic rays. If you've ever played with a bar magnet, you know it has a north pole and a south pole. It's the same with Earth. The north magnetic pole is located near the North Pole, and the south magnetic pole is near the South Pole (though it hasn't always been that way). Without our magnetic sphere, life on Earth would be difficult, if not impossible. The solar wind would eat away our atmosphere, and dangerous radioactive particles would strike us. Earth has a magnetic field because the core of our planet contains molten iron. As this liquid metal churns around, it creates electric currents, which produce magnetic forces.

What about the Moon? Scientists believe that the Moon once had a strong magnetic field. This was several billion years ago, when the Moon may have had flowing liquid metal in its core. Scientists found evidence of this former magnetic field in rocks that astronauts brought back from the Moon's surface. Today, however, the Moon doesn't have a magnetic field. The Moon's core may contain liquid iron, but scientists believe it's no longer churning around. We may have the Moon to thank for our own magnetic field, however. Some scientists believe that the tidal forces created by the Moon's gravity are part of what has kept the iron in Earth's core flowing.[1]

---

[1] Andrault, D., J. Monteux, M. Le Bars, and H Samuel. "The deep Earth may not be cooling down." Earth and Planetary Science Letters, 443 (1 June 2016), 195-203.

Are there auroras on the Moon?

Answer:

On Earth, auroras are beautiful streaks of multicolored light in the night sky that appear near the poles in the northern hemisphere (we sometimes call them the northern lights), and the southern hemisphere (the southern lights). If you live far enough north or south, you might have seen them. They look like glowing, rippling curtains in the sky. Auroras are caused by the solar wind—a stream of tiny, high-energy particles the Sun is constantly sending toward us. When this solar wind hits Earth's magnetic field, the particles interact with molecules in Earth's atmosphere, which release energy in the form of light.

The solar wind also flows over our Moon, but we know that the Moon doesn't have an atmosphere—at least, not one nearly thick enough to produce auroras. We also know the Moon doesn't have a magnetic field. So no, you couldn't watch auroras on the Moon. You'd still have a beautiful view of planet Earth in the lunar sky, though.

What if we had a lunar high jump competition? Who would win?

Due to the Moon's lower mass, gravity on the Moon is only about one-sixth as strong as gravity on Earth. That means a person weighing 120 lbs (54 kg) on Earth would weigh only 20 lbs (9 kg) on the Moon. It also means that you could jump a lot higher. Think about how high you can jump on Earth before gravity pulls you back down. Maybe a foot or two. On the Moon, you'd be able to jump six times as high and stay up for longer. Imagine jumping 10 feet up before falling down again. You'd feel like you were flying.

So who would win a high jump competition on the Moon? The world record for high jumping on Earth is currently about 8 feet (2.45 m), set by Cuban athlete Javier Sotomayor in 1993. If Javier Sotomayor were to attempt that same jump on the Moon, he'd go up more than 48 feet (14.6 m). That's higher than a four-story building. He'd look like a super-hero!

Is it true that you can see the Great Wall of China from the Moon?

This is a myth. While the Great Wall of China is certainly big, and parts of it may be visible by spacecraft in low Earth orbit, it's not visible from the Moon which is about 239,000 miles (385,000 km) away from Earth. If you were viewing our planet from the Moon, Earth would look like a blue-and-white orb hanging in the sky. You'd be able to see oceans, continents, and clouds, but no human-made structures.

The Moon seems to shine very brightly. Why is it dark on Earth at night, and why don't we get a tan under the Moon?

Answer:

First, it's important to know that the Moon doesn't make light of its own. The glow we see from the Moon is actually sunlight reflecting off the Moon's surface. The Moon certainly looks bright sometimes, especially when it's full, but it's still nowhere near as bright as the source of its light, the Sun itself. In fact, the Sun is about 400,000 times as bright as the full Moon. That means we would have to some-how fit 400,000 Moons in the sky to equal the brightness of the Sun—imagine that! So you can't get a moon tan (or a moon burn), and even though the Moon is the brightest thing in the night sky, it's still quite dark at night.

Why does the Moon always look different – sometimes like a disk, sometimes like a slice of cheese, and sometimes like a thin sickle? Does it change all the time?

Answer:

Look up at the Moon tonight. If you can see it, notice what shape it is. If you go out again a couple of nights later, you'll see that the Moon looks slightly different—either a little rounder and fuller or a little smaller and thinner. What's going on?

To answer this, we have to remember two important things: that the Moon is constantly circling Earth and that the Moon shines with reflected light from the Sun. Whether we see the Moon as a full disk, a half-circle, or a tiny slice depends on where the Moon is in its orbit in relation to both Earth and the Sun.

When the Moon is directly between Earth and the Sun, you can't see it at all, because all of the Sun's light falls on the side of the Moon facing away from us. Even though the Moon is still there, you can't see it in the sky. This is called a new moon. It happens one day out of every month. As the Moon continues its orbit around Earth, you begin to see more of it. At first, the Moon appears as a thin sickle, like a fingernail clipping. It seems to grow larger and larger as the days pass. We call this a waxing (growing) crescent moon. When the Moon is at a 90 degree angle from Earth and the Sun, the Sun's light strikes half of the lunar surface we can see, and the Moon looks to us like a half-circle. We call this a first quarter moon. As the Moon continues to grow, it starts to look rounder and fuller, though it's still not a complete circle. We call this a waxing gibbous moon. Finally, when the Moon is on the side of Earth that is directly ▶

opposite the Sun, you can see the Sun's light on its full surface. This is the full moon—a big, round, glowing disk.

What happens after a full moon? Well, the process goes backwards. As the Moon continues to orbit Earth, you'll see a waning (shrinking) gibbous moon, a last quarter moon, a waning crescent moon, and then the Moon will disappear—it'll be a new moon again.

How can we distinguish a waning (shrinking) Moon from a waxing (growing) one?

The Moon goes through its phases so slowly that on any given night, it won't seem to change at all. How can you tell whether it's waning or waxing? As you look at the Moon, notice whether it's lit up on the right side or the left side. If you live in the northern hemisphere, the Moon lit up on its right side is waxing, and the Moon lit up on its left side is waning. For instance, if you see a crescent moon in the shape of a C, it's lit up from the left side—it's growing smaller. ▶

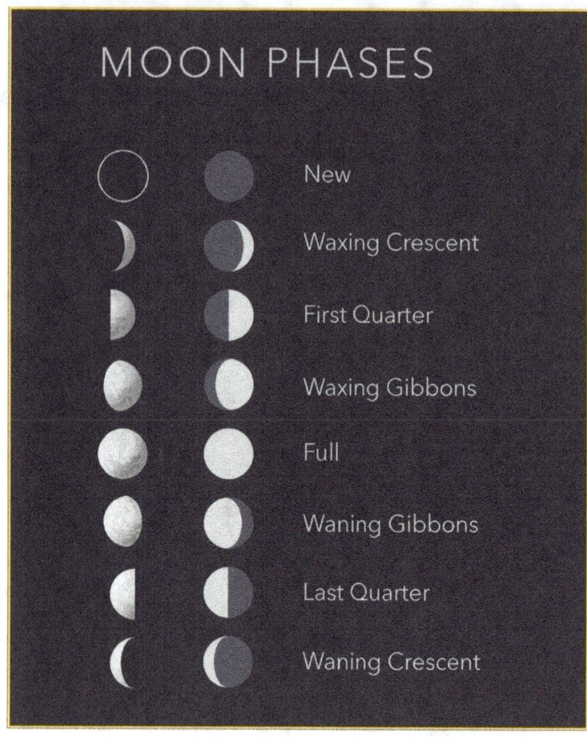

If you live in the southern hemisphere, the sides are reversed: a crescent moon in the shape of a C is waxing.

You can also tell whether the Moon is waxing or waning by looking at a lunar calendar.

What is the lunar calendar?

The eight phases of the Moon are: the new moon, waxing crescent, first quarter, waxing gibbous, full moon, waning gibbous, last quarter, and waning crescent. They repeat in a cycle that lasts roughly a month (29.5 days). We call this predictable cycle the lunar calendar. You're probably more familiar with the Gregorian Calendar, which goes from January to December and has 365 days in a year; this is the calendar that most of the world uses today, and it's based on the time it takes Earth to circle the Sun. A lunar month is a little shorter than most months (except February) on the Gregorian calendar. ▶

The lunar calendar is less common today, but it's still important. Some holidays are based on the lunar calendar. For instance, the Islamic holy month of Ramadan and the Hindu festival of Diwali begin around the time of the new moon. The lunar calendar is also useful for fishermen who need to keep track of tides and the Moon's brightness.

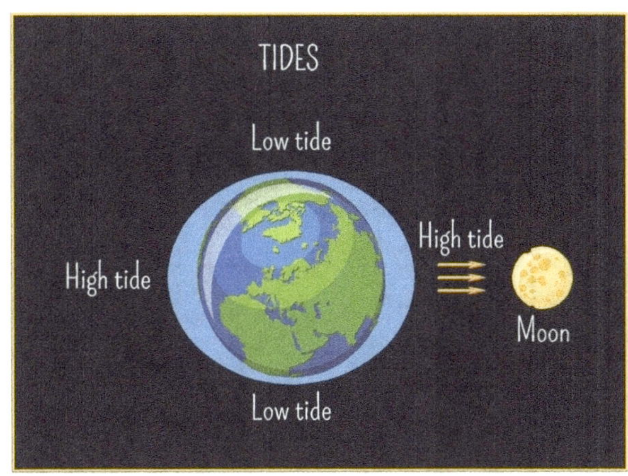

Question:

Why is the Moon sometimes visible in the daytime?

Answer:

When we think about the Moon, we usually picture it glowing at night. But you've probably noticed that the Moon sometimes comes out in the daytime, too. As a matter of fact, this happens a lot, but we often don't notice it because it's harder to see the Moon against the bright daytime sky. Why can we sometimes see the Moon and the Sun in the sky at the same time? ▶

It all depends on the Moon's phase. When the Moon is full, or directly opposite the Sun, we can't see it in the daytime—it rises at the same time the Sun is setting, and sets just as the Sun is rising, so we can only see it at night. But the other phases of the Moon rise and set at different times. Keep an eye open for the Moon next time you're outside during the day, and follow the lunar calendar. You're most likely to spot the first quarter moon (look in the afternoon) or the last quarter moon (look in the morning).

What is a supermoon?

You might have heard the word "supermoon." It's not a superhero (though that would be a fun name for one), nor is it the Moon with special powers. The supermoon is what we call a full moon that happens when the Moon is especially close to Earth.

The Moon's orbit around Earth is not actually a perfect circle. It's an ellipse, a shape like an oval. When the Moon is at its closest point to Earth, which we call its perigee, it's about 226,000 miles (364,000 km) away. When the Moon is at its furthest point from Earth, which we call its apogee, it's about 251,000 miles (404,000 km) away. A supermoon is a full moon ▸

when the Moon is at its perigee. It looks a little bigger and brighter in the sky than a regular full moon. As this usually only happens once or twice a year, a supermoon is a special event that you don't want to miss. You can keep track of the next supermoon by watching the news or astronomy websites.

What are solar and lunar eclipses? How do they happen?

Have you ever seen an eclipse? If so, you know it's an unusual and exciting sight. If not, you'll probably get to see one some day. Both solar and lunar eclipses are special celestial events that involve the Moon.

Solar eclipses, or eclipses of the Sun, happen when the Sun, Moon, and Earth are perfectly lined up and the Moon is between Earth and the Sun. This makes the Moon appear to cover up the Sun in the sky. During a total solar eclipse, you'll see the Moon creep over the Sun until the Sun is completely behind it. (Looking directly at a solar eclipse can damage your eyes, so you'll need to wear special glasses.) For a few minutes, it'll get as dark as night even though it's still daytime. You'll see the black disk of the Moon surrounded by a glowing ring of the Sun's light, called the corona. Then the Sun will start to come out again. A total solar eclipse can be dramatic to witness. More common is a partial solar eclipse, when the Moon only partly blocks the Sun.

Lunar eclipses happen more often than solar eclipses, and it won't hurt your eyes to look at them. ▶

They happen when Earth's shadow falls over the Moon, gradually making the Moon seem to disappear. This can only happen during a full moon, when the Moon is on the side of Earth opposite the Sun. Like solar eclipses, lunar eclipses can be total or partial. The change of light is less dramatic than a solar eclipse, but they can still be stunning to watch.

You can check astronomical websites, like NASA's, to learn the dates and times of future eclipses.

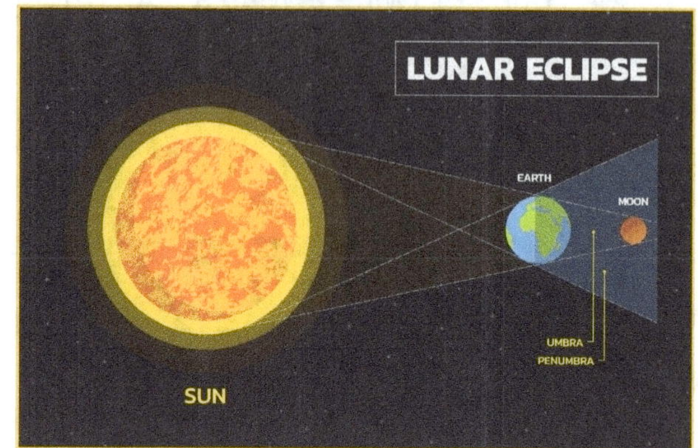

What are some famous historical eclipses?

Eclipses are awe-inspiring, unusual events, and they could be especially scary before people understood what caused them. Many cultures thought eclipses were signs from the gods. Sometimes they were believed to be omens (warnings of bad things to come).

In ancient China, people believed solar eclipses were warnings to the Emperor, who would perform rituals to try to bring back the sun. One such eclipse happened in 1302 B.C. A record from the time, which might be referring to the Sun's corona, reads "three flames ate the sun."[1]

In 1133, King Henry I of England died following a total solar eclipse. People at the time believed the eclipse was an omen of his death and of dark days for the country. Indeed, a civil war followed.

Christopher Columbus used a lunar eclipse in 1504 to trick the native people of Jamaica into believing he was powerful. He knew from consulting an almanac that a lunar eclipse was about to occur. ▶

---

[1] Liu, C., X. Liu, and Ma, L. "Examination of early Chinese records of solar eclipses." Journal of Astronomical History and Heritage, 6 (1), 2003, 53-63.

Columbus claimed the disappearance of the Moon was a sign that his god was angry and wanted the people of Jamaica to give his men more food and shelter.

Today, we know eclipses are natural events that happen when the Sun, the Moon, and Earth line up in a special way. While they may not be signs of death or disaster, they're still fascinating to watch.

Why does the Moon sometimes change its color?

Take a close look at the Moon the next time you see it. What color is it? We usually think of the Moon as white or yellowish, but sometimes it can take on a different hue. This is because of Earth's atmosphere, not the Moon itself.

During a total lunar eclipse, when the Moon is in Earth's shadow, the Moon can look reddish. This happens because Earth is blocking most sunlight from reaching the Moon. The light that does reach the Moon is filtered and scattered by Earth's atmosphere, and ends up looking red. This is sometimes called a blood moon, because of the blood-red

color. The Moon can also look reddish or orange when the sky is especially dusty or smoky or when the Moon is low on the horizon. ▶

This happens for a similar reason—because the light from the Moon is being scattered by Earth's atmosphere.

You may have heard the saying "once in a blue moon." A blue moon is what we call the second full moon in a (Gregorian) calendar month. It's unusual for there to be more than one full moon per month, but because the lunar calendar and the Gregorian calendar don't quite match, it happens every two or three years. Despite the name, a blue moon doesn't look blue—it looks just like a regular full moon.

Are the tides in the seas and oceans on Earth dependent on the Moon?

Yes, we have the Moon to thank for our tides. As the Moon orbits Earth, its gravity pulls on Earth's oceans, creating two bulges—one on the side of Earth facing the Moon, and one on the opposite side. As Earth spins on its axis, these bulges move over the coastlines, making the ocean level rise and fall throughout the day. If you've ever been to a beach at low tide, you might have had fun searching ▶

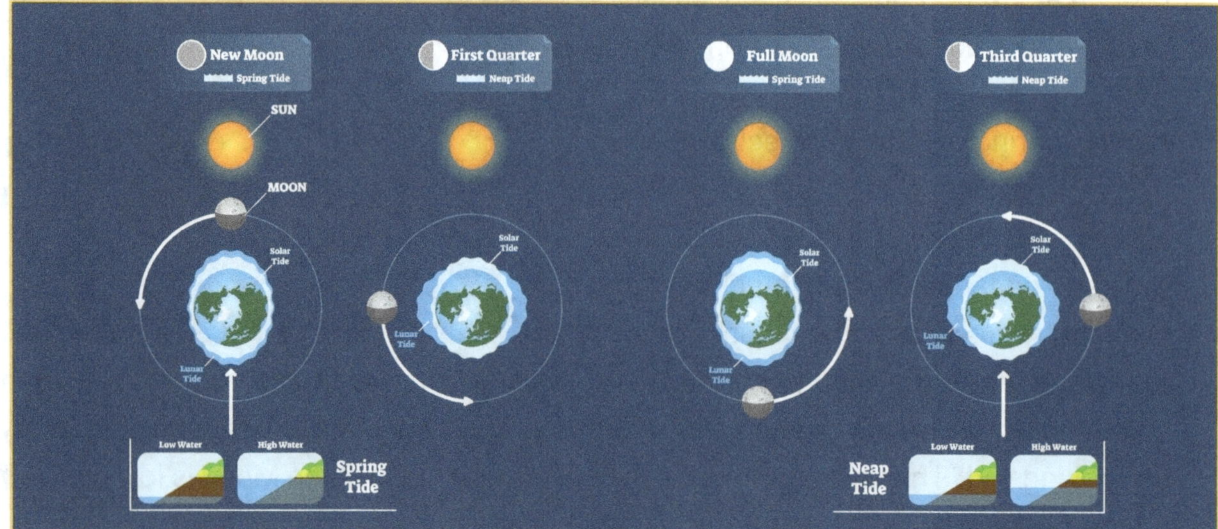

for crabs, starfish and other small sea animals living in tide pools. At high tide, the water rises and covers it all up. You'll have to wait a little over six hours for the tide to fall again.

Both the Moon and the Sun cause tides on Earth, but the Moon has a much stronger pull because it's so much closer to us. During full moons and new moons, when the Sun and Moon are lined up, their gravitational forces are working together. This makes tides more dramatic—high tides are higher and low tides are lower. These are called spring tides (though they happen during every season). The opposite is a weaker tide called a neap tide, which happens during first and third quarter moons.

How does the Moon slow Earth's rotation?

It might surprise you to learn that the Moon is part of why our days have 24 hours. When Earth first formed, 4.5 billion years ago, it spun on its axis much faster than it does today. This meant that days lasted only 5 or 6 hours rather than 24. Over billions of years, friction caused by the tides – which, remember, are due to the Moon's gravitational pull – slowed Earth's spinning little by little. Without the Moon, Earth would still have slowed down a little bit due to the pull of the Sun, but our days would be much shorter than 24 hours. Can you imagine trying to fit everything you do every day – eating meals, going to school, playing outside, doing hobbies and chores, and sleeping – into just 9 or 10 hours? You'd only have a few hours of daylight before the Sun would start to set again.

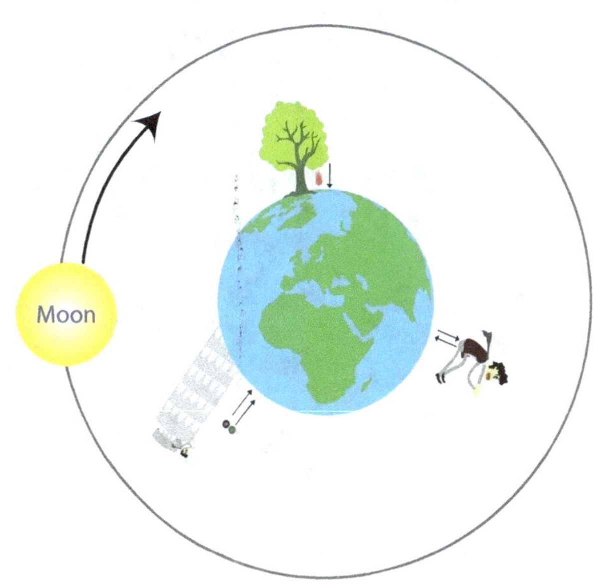

Can the Moon affect people's sleep?

There are a lot of myths and folktales about the Moon. You might have heard that the full moon can turn people into werewolves or cause madness (the word "lunacy" comes from Luna, the Latin name for the Moon). These are just myths, but other beliefs about the Moon might have some truth to them. One is that the full moon can make it harder for people to sleep, possibly because of how bright it is.

Researchers have found some scientific evidence to back up this idea. One study by Swiss scientists in 2013 looked at sleep habits among a group of 33 people[1]. The scientists found that people took longer to fall asleep and slept less deeply during the full moon. But the people in the study slept in a dark lab – they couldn't see the Moon's light. So if the full moon really was causing sleep problems, it could not have been because of the full moon's brightness. It's possible that our circadian rhythms (our bodies' natural sleep cycles) are in tune with the Moon's phases even if we can't see the Moon. ▶

---

[1] Cajochen, C., S. Altanay-Ekici, M. Münch, S. Frey, V. Knoblauch, and A. Wirz-Justice. "Evidence that the lunar cycle influences human sleep." Current Biology, 23(15), Aug 2013, 1485-8.

So does the Moon really affect our sleep? The answer is: It might, but we don't fully understand how. Maybe future studies will tell us more. In the meantime, if you're tossing and turning at night, you might be able to blame it on the full moon.

Does the Moon affect plant growth?

We know that plants need sunlight to grow. But can the Moon affect how plants grow, too? The answer isn't clear.

Throughout history and across cultures, many farmers and gardeners have paid attention to the Moon's phases as they planted crops. Some people still practice this ancient tradition of lunar gardening. One belief is that during a full moon, when the Moon and the Sun are lined up and their gravitational pulls are strongest (just as during a spring tide), moisture in the soil gets pulled upward and gives seeds the best chance to grow.

However, there isn't a lot of scientific evidence to back up these claims. More studies need to be done before we can say for sure whether the Moon affects plant growth. Maybe someday you'll conduct some of these studies yourself.

What if there were no Moon?

Imagine if Earth had never had a Moon. How would life be different for us? For one thing, you wouldn't be reading this book! Things would change in other ways, too. Think about this question for a few minutes before reading on. Given what you've read so far, can you think of any other ways life might be different without the Moon?

First of all, without the Moon to light up the night sky, nighttime would be darker, although we would be able to see more stars. The brightest object in the night sky would be the planet Venus, which is not nearly as bright as the Moon. You would have to be more careful when walking outside at night, and owls and other nocturnal animals would have a harder time hunting for food. The sky would be a little more boring, too—there would never be lunar eclipses (or solar ones, either).

Without the Moon, tides would be much smaller, and there would be fewer tide pools to explore. Our planet would spin faster and our days would be much shorter. Our calendars would look different, too. We would no lon-ger have January, February, March, or any of the months. These months were originally based on the time it takes the Moon to go through all of its phases. Without the Moon, we would have to divide up our years in a different way.

Can you think of any songs or poems about the Moon? What about myths or stories? We wouldn't have any of them. And, unless he became famous for something else, you would probably never have heard the name "Neil Armstrong."

Needless to say, our lives would be very different without the Moon. So the next time you see our natural satellite in the sky, remember how lucky we are to have it!

How did ancient people study the Moon?

Human beings have been studying the Moon for many thousands of years. Before the telescope was invented, people could only watch the Moon with their naked eyes. They observed the Moon's phases and the times when it rose and set, and sketched what they could see of its surface.

Some early astronomers held beliefs about the Moon that sound funny to us today. For instance, the ancient Greek philosopher Plutarch thought that there might be living beings on the Moon. Another well-known Greek astronomer, Aristotle, thought that the Moon was a perfectly smooth sphere. Others believed that there were seas of water on the Moon like there are on Earth. We now know these beliefs to be untrue, but early scientists were making their best guesses about the Moon based on what they could see. That would all change with a very important invention—the telescope.

In the sixteenth century, Italian astronomer Galileo invented the telescope. It was one of the most significant inventions in astronomy as it was the first time a person could observe the Moon so close. Galileo spent days and nights watching the Moon and making records. After months of observations, Galileo realized that the Moon was a satellite of the Earth and that it had its own mountains and valleys. The mystery of the Moon was disclosed in 1608.

Who invented the telescope, and how did this change what people knew about the Moon?

Answer:

If you've ever peered through a telescope, you know it makes objects in the sky look much bigger. The first telescope was invented in 1608 by a Dutch eyeglass-maker named Hans Lippershey. A year later, the famous Italian astronomer Galileo Galilei made his own telescope, which he used to study the night sky. He got a close-up view of the Moon's surface, including craters, mountains, and *maria*. This made it clear that the Moon was rough and rugged, not a smooth sphere as many people believed. Galileo also used his telescope to discover Europa, Ganymede, Callisto, and Io, the four largest moons of Jupiter. He published his findings in a book called *The Starry Messenger*. Galileo's discoveries were highly controversial at the time, as they conflicted with the teachings of the Catholic Church. Galileo was put on trial and found guilty of heresy (holding beliefs that challenge religious doctrine). Today, we know Galileo was right.

The telescope has come a long way since Galileo first used it to look at the Moon. Today, powerful tele-

scopes help scientists see stars, galaxies, and other objects in the distant universe. In 2019, a giant telescope called the Event Horizon Telescope, which is actually eight telescopes working together, let scientists see an image of a black hole for the first time ever.

Which space satellites were the first to go to the Moon?

Telescopes helped astronomers learn a lot about the Moon, but we learned even more when scientists from the Soviet Union and the United States began sending satellites there.

the Moon in 1966 and sent photographs of the lunar surface back to Earth. Over the next few years, several more Soviet and American satellites would land on or orbit the Moon.

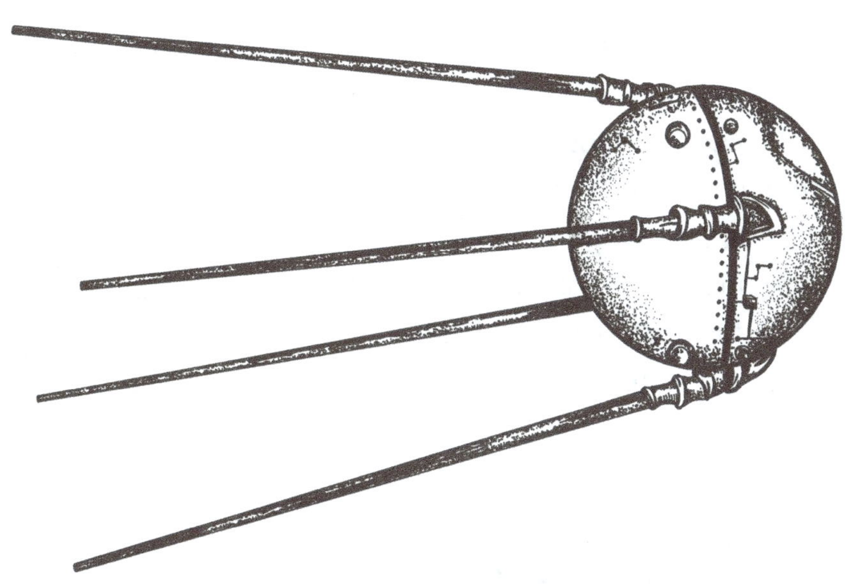

The first satellite to successfully reach the Moon's surface was called Luna 2. Scientists from the Soviet Union launched it in 1959. Luna 2 crashed-landed on the Moon (this was on purpose, as it didn't have the technology to land softly). The impact destroyed it, but Luna 2 showed the world that reaching the Moon was possible. Another Soviet spacecraft, Luna 9, landed softly on

None of these early satellites carried people on board. The first manned mission to the Moon was Apollo 8. This spacecraft, launched in 1968, carried three American astronauts. It circled the Moon 10 times and took many photographs before heading back to Earth.

Who was the first person to set foot on the Moon?

That would be the American astronaut Neil Armstrong, who landed on the Moon as part of the Apollo 11 mission on July 20, 1969. Armstrong famously called his first step on the Moon "one giant leap for mankind." Following behind him a few minutes later was his fellow astronaut, Buzz Aldrin. This incredible moment, which millions of people watched live on television, was the first time human beings had set foot on a world other than Earth. The astronauts spent more than two hours walking on the Moon's surface, taking photographs, conducting experiments, and collecting samples of the lunar soil, before going back to their spacecraft and preparing to return home.

Since Apollo 11, five other manned spacecraft have landed on the Moon, and ten other astronauts have walked there. Maybe someday you'll be the next.

The first person who walked on the Moon was Neil Armstrong. On 21 July 1969, Neil stepped out of his space shuttle. His first words were: "That is one small step for man, but one giant leap for mankind."

Do you know that there are no pictures of Mr. Armstrong on the Moon? There is only one picture where you can see Neil in the reflection of his partner's helmet.

Did any spacecraft fail to complete their missions?

Yes, quite a few of them failed. In the early days of the Soviet and American space programs, flying satellites into space was risky and there were many mistakes. You read that Luna 2 was the first spacecraft to reach the Moon's surface. An earlier Soviet spacecraft, Luna 1, wasn't so lucky. It missed the Moon and went off into space. In the late 1950s and 1960s, a number of other Soviet and American spacecraft either missed the Moon, crashed on it, or malfunctioned shortly after launching. These failures certainly must have been discouraging. Thankfully, scientists and engineers didn't give up. They continued working to design better rockets and spacecraft.

In 1970, a manned American spacecraft called Apollo 13 was supposed to land on the Moon, but things went very wrong. On the way there, an oxygen tank exploded, and oxygen began leaking into space. The three astronauts couldn't land on the Moon, but thankfully they were able to circle around it and return to Earth safely.

Later missions have had a higher success rate, but it's not 100 percent. In 2019, an Israeli satellite called Beresheet crashed when it tried to land on the Moon, demonstrating that lunar exploration is still risky.

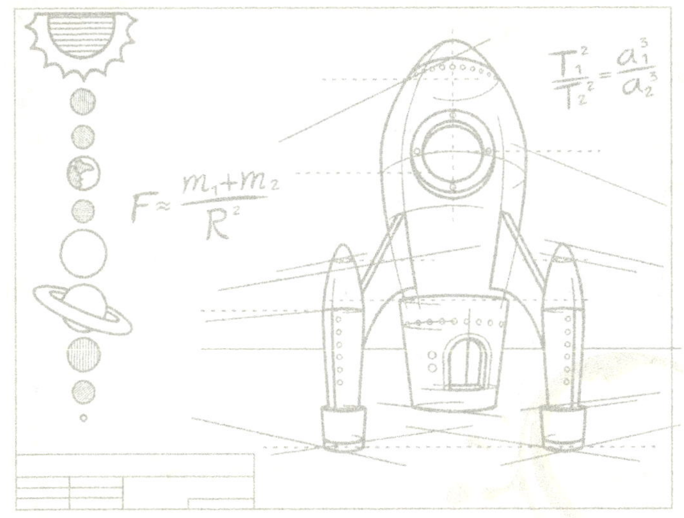

What happens to Moon rovers that are out of order?

What's even more fun than walking on the Moon? Driving a car on it! Moon rovers, or lunar rovers, are vehicles that drive across the surface of the Moon. Astronauts used them during the Apollo 15, 16, and 17 missions. They looked a little like dune buggies and weren't very fast--their top speed was about 8 mph (13 km/hr)--but they allowed astronauts to explore more of the Moon than they could have on foot. These three rovers are still on the Moon, since there was no easy way of getting them home.

Rovers don't have to carry astronauts. Soviet scientists sent robotic, remote-controlled rovers to the Moon in 1970 and 1973. These rovers, named Lunochod 1 and Lunochod 2, are still on the surface of the Moon. They beamed back data and images for several months before they stopped working. In recent years, Chinese scientists have sent two robotic rovers to the Moon. The first, called Yutu, was part of the Chang'e-3 mission in 2013. It was a small rover that carried scientific instruments and was pow- ▶

ered by solar panels. It malfunctioned and stopped moving soon after landing on the Moon, but it continued to send data back to Earth for more than two years. In 2019, another rover named Yutu 2 landed on the far side of the Moon as part of the Chang'e-4 mission. Like the Apollo and Lunochod rovers, these little rovers will probably stay on the Moon's surface forever—unless future astronauts decide to bring them home.

How long does it take to fly from Earth to the Moon?

The answer is—it depends on how fast you go. On average, the Moon is about 239,000 miles (385,000 km) away from Earth. It took the Apollo 11 astronauts about three days to reach the Moon, and another day to land on its surface. That's an average speed of over 3,000 mph (4,800 kmh). By comparison, if you were to somehow drive a car to the Moon at 70 mph (113 kmh), it would take you over 4 months to get there. That's a long road trip! So far, the fastest spacecraft to reach the Moon was the New Horizons space probe, launched by NASA in 2006, which passed by the Moon on its way to Pluto 8.5 hours after leaving Earth. This spacecraft wasn't trying to land on the Moon, so it didn't have to slow down.

What is weightlessness?

Weightlessness is the floating feeling that astronauts experience while in space. If you've ever jumped from something high, or been on a roller coaster or other amusement park ride, you've probably felt a few moments of weightlessness yourself. It's actually a form of free-falling, and it can be both fun and disorienting (and sometimes even nauseating at first). The Apollo astronauts experienced weightlessness on their way to the Moon. You would too, unless you were in a spacecraft that had some sort of artificial gravity that kept your feet on the floor. Once you arrived on the Moon's surface, you would no longer be weightless, but you would weigh only one-sixth of what you weighed on Earth.

Weightlessness can cause health problems for astronauts who spend a lot of time in space. This is because the bones and muscles of the body start to weaken without the pull of gravity. A three-day flight to the Moon probably wouldn't cause you much trouble, but what if you stayed there for months or years? It's unclear how living on the Moon long-term might affect people's health. It's likely that you would need to do a lot of daily exercise to keep your body strong.

Why do we no longer fly astronauts to the Moon? Are people no longer interested in our satellite?

Answer:

The last time human beings were on the Moon was in 1972, during the Apollo 17 mission. We've never gone back, and it's only natural to wonder why.

It isn't that people aren't interested in the Moon anymore. Most of the explanation simply has to do with cost. It's expensive and risky to fly people to the Moon. During the 1950s and 1960s, leaders in the United States and the Soviet Union were motivated to spend a lot of money on their space programs because they were in competition with each other—a time of rivalry sometimes called the "space race." Today, there's less pressure for the U.S. government (or other governments) to invest the amount of money it would take to send people back to the Moon.

But does this mean that people will never go back to the Moon? We certainly wouldn't say that. Some scientists think the Moon might be a good place to train astronauts for future missions to Mars. There are also private corporations interested in sending people to the Moon. As of 2019, NASA is developing plans to work with private companies to send equipment, rovers, and eventually people back to the Moon. Other countries, including China and Russia, and the European Space Agency are also working on plans to send people to the Moon. If these plans succeed, the next few years could be very exciting for lunar exploration. It's impossible to know the future, but there's a good chance that human beings will indeed walk on our natural satellite again.

What has changed since people started flying into space?

Technology has come a long way since people started flying into space in the 1960s. Engineers learned from early launch failures how to build better and more powerful rockets to carry spacecraft into Earth's orbit and beyond. Computers are also much more advanced today. The computers scientists used during the early years of the U.S. and Soviet space programs were the size of a room and were much slower and less powerful than the computers you're used to. Today, advanced computer technology helps scientists program and control the flight paths of spacecraft with precision.

There have been other changes, too. We've learned a lot more about the effect of weightlessness on the human body and what it takes to keep people living in space for long periods of time. Our knowledge about space has grown—we've sent satellites to other planets and built stronger telescopes that can see farther into the universe. Space exploration today also involves more international cooperation than it once did. A great example of this is the International Space Station, or ISS, which was built by the United States, Russia, Canada, Japan, and eleven European countries.

Could we build a space elevator to the Moon?

Imagine if going to the Moon were as simple as stepping into an elevator cab and pushing a button. If a long enough cable stretched from Earth to the Moon, it could, in theory, carry you all the way there. A space elevator wouldn't necessarily have to stretch the whole way to the Moon, either. A space elevator might carry you from the ground to some point in space high above Earth. From there, you could get into a ship and go to the Moon without having to use a lot of rocket fuel escaping from Earth's gravity.

Sounds like science fiction, doesn't it? But some scientists think a space elevator might be a reality someday. It would cost a lot to build one, but once it was in place, getting people into space—and possibly to the Moon—would be cheaper and easier. A group of scientists and organizations called the International Space Elevator Consortium (ISEC) is currently researching the technology we would need to build a space elevator. Some of the challenges include how to build a cable or tether strong enough to stretch into space and how to protect the elevator against rocks and debris that might strike

it. We may not see a space elevator in the next few years, but it's an exciting possibility for the future.

Could we put solar panels on the Moon?

A solar panel operates by collecting energy from the Sun and converting it to electricity. Some scientists have suggested putting solar panels on the Moon and using the energy from them to power things on Earth. Because the Moon doesn't have clouds to get in the way, solar panels would collect sunlight constantly during the long lunar days. A Japanese company called Shimizu, for instance, is working on a project called the Luna Ring—a ring of solar panels stretching all the way around the Moon's equator.[1] These panels would collect energy from the Sun and beam it back to Earth. Because half of the Moon is always in daylight, half of the panels would always be gathering energy. The Luna Ring could potentially meet the energy needs of our entire planet. This would be a costly and challenging project, and now it's still just an idea. But it's exciting to think about how solar panels on the Moon might be able to solve our energy problems here on Earth.

[1] Ryall, J. "Japanese firm plans 250 mile-wide solar panel belt around Moon." The Telegraph, 28 Nov. 2013. <https://www.telegraph.co.uk/news/worldnews/asia/japan/10480950/Japanese-firm-plans-250-mile-wide-solar-panel-belt-around-Moon.html>

Where should I start if I want to become a resident of the Moon someday?

Answer:

If you want to go to the Moon someday, your best bet is to become an astronaut. This requires a lot of education and training. For instance, to become a NASA astronaut, you'll need a bachelor's degree in engineering, biological science, physical science, computer science, or math, plus at least 1,000 hours of experience piloting a jet aircraft or three years of similar experience.[1] You'll also need to pass a physical exam to make sure your body can handle the stress of being in space. If selected, you'll go through a two-year training program. Becoming an astronaut doesn't necessarily mean you'll be sent to the Moon, but you'll be ready to go if the opportunity comes. Being an astronaut is an exciting, adventurous, highly challenging career that's not right for everyone, but it may be for you!

There are lots of other ways to help people explore the Moon without becoming an astronaut. You could become a scientist who studies the Moon or an engineer who helps design satellites,

---

[1] NASA. "Astronaut requirements." 21 June 2017.
<https://www.nasa.gov/audience/forstudents/postsecondary/features/F_Astronaut_Requirements.html>

lunar rovers, or even space elevators. Your discoveries could help put people on the Moon someday. You'll need an advanced college degree in astronomy, physics, computer science, or engineering, so be sure to work hard in school.

Summing up

As we reach the end of this book, reflect back on all you've learned about Earth's natural satellite. You've learned about the Moon's size and weight, its distance from us, and how it orbits Earth. You've learned about the mountains, craters, and "seas" on the Moon's dusty surface. You've learned what causes eclipses, why the Moon sometimes appears full and sometimes doesn't appear at all, and you've learned what a supermoon is. And you've learned about the history of human exploration of the Moon as well as some exciting possibilities for the future. We hope that this book has been an interesting and thought-provoking journey. The next time you see Earth's natural satellite in the sky, give it a wave. It's been there for all of human history, and it'll continue to awe and inspire us for as long as we're here to gaze up at it.